An Exploration of a Case of Nervous Being

(2009)

*

also:
A Few Related Concepts

*

essay

*

Traumear

Contents:

*

1

Dealing with a case of bad nerves by building a reserve of courage for the future. It contains valuable insights into humanity in comparison to popularity.

*

An Exploration of a Case of Nervous Being

Some annoyances have a way of habitually throwing us off balance. It is as if we were doomed to an almost ritualistic confrontation with insuperable odds. In the face of certain uncertain experiences we find again and again that we simply cannot cope. We do not cope, and surely this means that we cannot cope. We have made a habit of reacting rather than responding.

The first instance of our sensing that something is going wrong is an occasion of nervous being. I am being nervous. This is the first stage. The next stage is: I am afraid something highly unpleasant is about to happen. Along with this comes the sad realization that we cannot escape. A mechanical necessity has taken hold of us and going by past experience, 'we are in for it now'. Guilt may or may not play a role. Even if it does, there is no guarantee of it being justified. We may simply feel guilty for not being able to deal with what seems to be coming our way, or for still not having worked out a solution to this problem.

Nervous being can have many causes. Should we study these supposed causes and feel proud of ourselves or should we instead study the experience itself and find out where it leads us, in the hope of building something like a reserve of courage that will allow us to deal profitably with future occasions of it? I prefer the latter.

*

We find ourselves in situations where we can no longer behave normally. It appears that our behaviour is taking over with a will of its own, so that we say or do what we regret having said or done afterwards. We did not know what we were doing. What was it that interrupted our knowing? We are accused of having been unkind, cruel, malicious and all we can say in hindsight is that we intended no such thing. We did not even intend. Consequently we fail to see how we can be held responsible for any consequences.

The hard truth of the matter is that we are responsible not only for what we do and say intentionally but equally for what we do and say unintentionally. As we mature, this is increasingly the case.

At this stage we need to remind that spontaneous saying and doing is not unintentional but rather the intention coincides precisely with the speech and action. Spontaneity is betimes confused with a lack of forethought or care.

We are careless when our nerves are not properly invested in our being. At the same time there is such a thing as an enervating experience. There are activities which, if we involve ourselves in them, seem pleasant at the time but they affect us by weakening our character. Such for example are all indulgences in virtual entertainment when the intention is cynical rather than conscientious. A discussion of character would therefore throw light on what we mean by strong nerves.

*

A lot of our feeblenesses, as we get older, are really cases of nerve failure. We become lazily comfortable, there are fewer external challenges and as a consequence we see no further need for exercising our faculties.

At the same time we know that a human being always grows. We grow towards maturity and we grow in maturity. Now since human growth is and remains a cooperation of ourselves in spirit with our human nature, we should never really expect a time when our creative input is no longer required.

The requirements differ, of course, from one time to the next and from one person to the next. Therefore the question that pertains specifically to our nerve-strength is: How can I help? This is the question we will ask in spirit and in truth, so that this particular side of our personality will not diminish or become detrimentally involved in enervating activity or passivity. How can I help, so that my presence at this stage of my life will be exemplary and not self-indulgent?

Not until I ask this question, in spirit and truth, which is to say in reality, do I become aware of challenges that pertain specifically to my nerve-system, so that next I may ask: What might be the most profitable way of meeting these challenges?

The assumption of a *nerve-system* amounts in itself to nerves under stress. Systems are always defensive measures. If we can hold out for a time confronted with the realization that our nerves are compromised, that they tend to slacken rather than to spring into action as soon as need arises, then for that time we build a new source of *nerve-power*. This is something quite new and well worthy of our consideration in detail.

3

By power we always imply good effectiveness. Nerve-power specifically widens and deepens our effectiveness during personal relation and communication.

*

It is ultimately desirable to be able to cope successfully with whatever comes our way during personal intercourse. The passive capacity of our soul is as important as its active ability. Nerve-power pertains specifically to our willingness to undergo, to be receptive and inclusive. The more readily we can accept, the fewer prejudices and principles do we need.

Not *what* we accept but *that* we accept concerns us here. In the absence of nerve-power we experience whatever is extended towards us as a risk of intrusion. The physiology of what we extend towards others and in general towards our environment may be finely worked out. We have our principles to let us know what is right and what is wrong and according to them we judge. How these principles arise in the first place does not concern us here. As for hasty responses, when we find ourselves pressed, that is where our prejudices come in and rarely do we recognize them as such in ourselves, though more readily in others.

What I am describing here is a one-sided way of being and behaving, specifically one-sided in favour of outer experience and of activity we initiate and in which we participate. Calling it at best principled and prejudicial underlines the inner weakness, the comparative inability to respond creatively to challenges from outside. A ready supply of nerve-power obviates any reliance on principles and prejudices.

Needless to say, what we want is equal resources of nerve- and muscle power, keeping in mind we are describing our operational soul. I see no reason why we should not employ the term 'voluntary' and 'involuntary' here too. A materialistic mind-set presents us with the greatest difficulties of understanding here. It should help us to keep in mind that in the absence of soul, human being is inconceivable. Also, psyche is not soul but soul in distress or, metaphorically expressed, a shadow of our soul.

On contemplating a piece of literature we might refer to 'muscular prose'. How telling, that we rarely hear anyone refer to 'nervy prose'. Great poetry too should be both muscular and nervy. The same goes for great human being. Do we not wish we did not jump to conclusions, did not overreact or exaggerate, did not grow emotionally timid, did not insist on being right for fear of being proved wrong, did not judge so as not to be judged? If that or any part of it is our wish, we can benefit from knowledge of what it means to be nervy, to be strong in nerve and sinew and to be in the possession of a soul that does not shirk the burdens of spiritual growth, does not shrink from its challenges.

*

Nerves thrive on fear.

On the surface of it, this sounds ridiculous. Is fear not precisely a sign of our losing our nerve? The point is this: By holding out in the face of fear rather than opting for fight or flight we improve our nerves. In our youth we might even choose to expose ourselves to danger of one sort or another because we sense that by overcoming fear we grow stronger. What we may not understand until later is that the danger to which we voluntarily expose ourselves is not the same as the danger of the unfamiliar territory into which we human-naturally grow. The most intrepid adventurer is reduced to a state of morbid timidity, to which he cruelly overreacts, when he returns to his wife and children.

It is the fear we encounter in ourselves during the natural course of daily events that affords us beneficial exercise for our nerves – once again, inasmuch as we hold out rather than shirking and shrinking, rather than accusing and blaming.

While awaiting the next bout of fear, the next onset of a 'panic attack' – there are those who will know exactly what I mean – is there anything we can do in terms of preparedness and readiness? A timid nature is not complete, that goes without saying. Poor decisions and hasty reactions arise from it. The man who said: 'We have nothing to fear except fear itself' must have meant something like that. Sadly he did not go on to inform us how to deal with that fear of fear, that vicious circle of a destructive mentality.

It puts me in mind of what someone else said about fear: 'Do not fear those who can kill the body and not the soul but rather the one who can destroy both body and soul in hell.'[1]

---

[1] Christian Bible: Mat. 10:28

It would appear that we can fear intentionally. This is not generally known in a materialistic age that builds its hopes on everlasting happiness. We might do well to reflect on this business of intentional fear, on one side and of fear that happens, on the other. Or let's differentiate between rational and irrational fear first. Rational fear spurs us on to action that will avert the danger. Irrational fear, such as of ghosts or of other sources of superstition, is self-imposed and can only be cured if we rid ourselves of superstition, which, mind you, is easier said than done.

There is however a third kind of fear and this is the one that pertains to our desire for strong nerves. We do not experience it unless we have a soul. I do not mean unless we are theologically persuaded that surely, by definition, we must have a soul because we believe those who say they know better than we do but rather unless we know in truth and from physical experience that our soul, our sense of whole being, is our most valuable possession and that we may lose possession of it and end in misery.

This fear, that we may lose our soul and that it may be taken from, us is healthy enough. It too may come upon us uninvited, perhaps as a reminder, a wake-up call. It too is a rational fear, in that it spurs us on to behave in some remedial fashion or simply to secure ourselves. Here however the action we are to take is exclusively to fear intentionally, in the knowledge that unless we do so, our soul is in danger. We are to fear the one who has power over our soul. This means first of all realizing that such a one exists and secondly it means understanding that the one we mean has jurisdiction over our most precious possession, which alone makes anything else worth possessing.

Now we know what we can do to help ourselves while we are not presently in the grips of this particular fear. We can reflect on the fact that not only can we possess our soul, we are also liable to lose it. We can practice being mindful of the one who has power over our soul. Dwelling on such knowledge builds up our nerve-fibre. If we wait every time until we are struck by fear – by panic, by terror – we may find it tricky enough to distance ourselves from this all-embracing emotion, while rational thought or true knowing may not come readily, if it comes at all, simply because right from he start we lose our nerve.

Add to this the fact that the fear I mean here is not readily even recognized as fear and the complexities mount. There are those who lack confidence. Some are driven in their daily lives by what they do not understand. So this fear may be an undercurrent of their daily existence while they are far from recognizing it as such. Schooled in materialist thought, we look only for external and internal causes, for grizzly bears and cancer, for burglars and despots. We only know what we can point out to one another.

Modern thinking and feeling makes room for supernatural phenomena, for spiritual entities of whatever sort, and the fear we mean here, that enervates unless we intend it intelligently, appertains physiologically to whole human beings; to men, women and children. Not man, not the human being, but individual human beings pay the cost at times when this fear is upon them, lacerating, destroying any incarnate good spirit in their possession. It feels like hell. It is always at least a little bit like going through hell. Of course incarnate spirit as such cannot be destroyed but rather our hold on it, our beholding of it, and that is what counts for us.

Identification of this enervating fear is therefore half the battle. Personally I know of no one who is not at least subconsciously affected by it, if not downright familiar with it. There is the almost pathological insecurity of which so many speak when they dare to converse intimately. There is the sense that nowhere is certainty to be maintained. There is one anxiety, that we may not be able to complete the task allotted to us in the available time and this is perfectly rational. What about that other anxiety for which we can find no reason? Why is such a great percentage of the population taking drugs of one sort or another, as if sobriety were never entirely supportable?

It's no use waiting for Society to accommodate us. We can only succeed if we take responsibility for our own existence, otherwise we have nothing worthwhile to offer to others.

There is no accounting for the innumerable guises this unknown fear takes on, mostly because it is unknown and unknowable. Some have called it the ontological fear, the fear of being. Since we cannot know it, we pretend we do. Some are afraid of spiders, others of being alone and still others of just plain living. Of course spiders, solitude and life have nothing to do with it. These are just masks our unconscious fear produces. They quickly fall off as soon as we intend to fear. Fear what? Fear whom?

What is a human soul? What is it that allows us to be whole and undivided? What makes us secure in ourselves and confident, in a crowd or in front of a crowd? What is it that allows us to communicate intimately with another human being or two? Whence this sense that we 'contain multitudes'?

When social status and prestige fall away, what are we left with?

In an age when we all depend more and more on machines, when thinking and feeling are externalized and internalized, and consequently increasingly trivialized, when so many of our activities, our 'jobs', are soul-destroying, should we not reasonably expect this simultaneous 'fear of the soul', or 'fear for our soul'?

My soul as physiologically real is something I can barely talk about to anyone nowadays. The Christians have turned it into a generality and an abstraction, indeed for the up-to-date Christian it is nothing more than the psyche. However we cannot learn the attributes of a whole man by observing a sick individual.

So how are we expected to believe, that this debility and general impotence that besets us, this decadence that turns up as the result of many a respectable diagnosis, is really our fear for our soul, if we have no notion of the reality, the physical reality, in terms of our mind and body, of soul-being?

Oh, we have heard of the soul as a thing, even as a thing-in-itself, believe it or not, as those theologians who deal in things would have us believe. The soul as operation, as work, is largely still unknown. The modern spirit could never conceive of it, being modern. It reacts to it, sentimentally or cynically.

It would make an interesting study, if we had too much time on our hands, this modern reaction of fight or flight to contemporary soul-knowledge. We have to stop being modern if we want to repossess our soul.

And let's not pretend that children are immune to soul-destruction and soul-malignity. No more crucial task exists for both child-education and adult-education than this raising of awareness of the soul we were once familiar with, perhaps as far back as the cradle.

Let me see now if I can return to my topic.

It seems we cannot know this 'existentialist' fear for what it really amounts to, unless we know our soul, and conversely we cannot repossess our soul, unless we learn to fear, intentionally, the spiritual entity that would, if we deserve it, cast us body and soul into the waste-bin of extinction.

How we struggle so as not to be discarded and how our very efforts in that direction defeat our purpose!

How fortunate for us, if we experience dissatisfaction with our soul in danger, our soul at risk!

There is that which can harm our body and that which can harm our body and soul.

There is that which can harm our mind and that which can harm our mind and soul.

What concerns us here is not that which can harm our body or our mind, which we face with courage, but that which can harm our body and soul, our mind and soul, which we face with fear, perhaps with fear and trembling.

At first perhaps only our courage needs to be tested. Our soul may be intact though not at all familiar to us as such. Proper upbringing and expedient education shall make us aware of our soul. We shall know our body and our mind and we shall also know our soul.

There may be doubt as to how our body and our mind can really be ours and not just traditional by-products of institutional being. Then the soul-connection of both our mind and our body will be tested. How indeed can we own a body and a mind, how can they be ours, if their soul-connection has become precarious, if their dependence on a soul is gone? The horror of it!

Let us meanwhile keep in mind that what concerns us her is a clinical understanding of some of the horrors and terrors that will encumber a creative personality, which includes knowing how to confront them productively.

We are not made afraid so that we will run or resist but so that we will be repaired. When I say 'we are made afraid', I take for granted that the spirit of which we are afraid is powerful in our interest. In other words the source of the fear is not a malicious agency but a growth-energy. It's up to us to recognize it as such. Principally then there are two ways to do this. We notice we are beset by an insecurity that makes us ill. We feel exposed, lost, neglected, rejected and our 'health is suffering'. We are pathologically affected by negative states of mind or soul. Let our response to this be, that we fear the agency or spirit that brings these states about in us, as we have learned. We do not fear the states but that which (or the one who) has caused them. Of course we have to be capable of fear as an action and not merely a blind reaction. We can take it for granted however that if this fearful, isolating, energy has accessed us we must be worthy of it. This is the 'good news' we may take on board. If we are too afraid to accept this good news, we need a good talking to. Needless to say, I am incorporating such a 'talking-to' in this present essay.

You may also be beset by ailments of the body that no one can make head or tail of. Doctors guess this way and that and only shake their heads. If you are not careful, the less conscientious ones among them will use you as an experiment or as a practice session. Get a hold of yourself. Your condition is not medically treatable. Besides, nothing or no one can scare or bully or coax you into doing what is needful here. You have to understand what is going on. And then you must do the needful. Whatever it is that bothers you, in body or mind or soul, is a wake-up call to a needful growth-orientation, which you need to effect.

So learn how to fear. You have learned how to love, how to worship in the spirit and in truth, how to care where care is needed in particular. You have learned how to ask for what you know you have already. Now learn how to fear. *As soon as you fear you will cease being afraid.* As soon as you swim you will stop sinking. Learn how to swim.

*

It would be interesting if someone could study, with some of these electronic instruments people come up with these days, the material effect this intentional fear has on our so called nervous system. Ask yourself who you look up to. Is it someone who is greater than you, smarter, stronger or more beautiful? No reason to fear anyone like that. Now here is someone who can take your soul away and who might just do that unless you recognize his power. He won't do it out of malice but rather he couldn't help do that because he has to stimulate your human growth in the only way he can and if you don't play the game he can't very well be someone else or do otherwise than he does by definition. He is the creative spirit and if you don't go ahead and create, his effect cannot help but be destructive. So there you have it. I don't say that fear is supposed to be your only approach but it's very easy for a creative human being to get bigger than his boots and don't we know from Greek tragedy where that leads. Playwrights through the ages have often reminded us of this uncaring, high-fallutin' strain in our nature, especially if we have a lot of talent and perhaps even genius. It is madness not to have anyone to look up to. Those who are rich in spirit are in especial danger of overreaching themselves. The man who said 'I hope nothing, I fear nothing, I am free' was surely speaking politically.

It is by way of our nerves that we register the demands made on us by creative spirit. Our nerves, alas, are not intelligent. They tell us what happens but not what we must do. We do well to reflect on this. Creative spirit does not influence us when we suppose it should, to please us; it pleases itself, in our better interest.

How does creative spirit appear to us if we ignore its demands? It appears as critical spirit. Critical spirit is creative spirit ignored or misunderstood by us. The crisis critical spirit refers to is our soul at risk. Of course we may discern this spirit too but we must know that when we come upon it, the time has advanced. We are liable, now, to believe in the reality of this critical spirit when in fact it appears as a result of our ignorance and misunderstanding. The critic lives on his nerves. For him, creative spirit is not a being and it has no being but it is a thing, and this thing, in fact now critical spirit, implies soullessness. The smirk of the cynic, the cold stare of the materialist, bear testimony to this soulless state. Both are guilty of externalized reactions. Internalized, by comparison, are the reactions of the sentimentalist and the idealist while the realist's reaction is not flight but fight.

It is not contempt of error, however, that returns us to the true path but the dread of our ignorance and the alarm at our misunderstanding and in turn the fact that we stand in awe of the spirit that inspires and guides us as we benefit one another and from one another.

The communality of creative spirit should wonderfully persuade us, for we know we can be as great but not greater than our master.

*

Again, how can anyone tell us to fear and what to fear? Surely fear happens, at one with a supposed or real danger.

The etymological meaning of 'fear' points to any danger encountered while travelling, so in the German,

15

for example, we have 'fahren', to travel, 'Gefahr', danger and 'Furcht', fear. It helps us, then, to think of human beings as on a path, on the road, voyaging. As travellers in life, towards more life, for what are we wise to look out? I mean travellers, on a journey, not tourists, who are static individuals shunted from place to place by the latest accomplishments of technology.

Neither are we passive or accidental travellers, we human beings. Each of us has a specific journey mapped out for him (or her). We have to keep our wits about us so as not to go off the road into the ditch; so as to outwit the highwayman and to see the holes or boulders that make stretches of road seemingly impassable. The task we set ourselves is the task that is set for us, for we cherish freedom. Whatever runs counter to the truth curbs our freedom. Our liberty we curb ourselves, for the sake of the task in hand.

Now some dangers on the road are to life and limb, while others would only slow us down for an hour or a day. Without labouring the metaphor, do we agree that care deals with the latter but fear is required for the former?

We fear. We revere. We know, because we have experienced, what happens when we ignore the creative spirit. That is what we fear and that is what keeps us on our toes. Misunderstandings are readily corrected but total ignorance, unwillingness to countenance, is a stupidity that draws down the most dire consequences. Correction to body or mind is an easy matter. Commonly an increase in intelligent trust, which springs from our soul, deals with the matter in hand. But what if our soul itself needs to be corrected? The total misery and despair that is our lot then is not to be countenanced. We may give ourselves up for lost and throw ourselves on the bosom of the creator, for whom we have deep respect and awe.

*

It is our destiny to grow. We understand nothing about human beings unless we take account of that. Every day, from sunrise to nightfall, we may interpret our experience and behaviour in terms of our destiny and that way we thrive. As materialists we are suspicious of what we cannot see, what we cannot lay our hands on. So we demand a sign before we believe and accept the value of something. We husband our plants and animals by giving them what they need; shelter, water, food and light. Human beings need and want more than these because our humanity requires, our human being needs, something that is not covered by shelter, water, food and light. In no other beings is the human spirit aware of itself. The human spirit that is borne by us when we are born requires and needs from us that we know and understand it. It bears the most minute and insightful investigation, by me in me and by you in you. The ancient 'know yourself' became the modern 'know what you are', however for contemporary men and women the command is 'know who you are', and knowledge in all three cases is different. For the ancients knowledge was a case of 'observe yourself and draw some hard conclusions'.[1] This principle is honoured especially in the earlier tragedies of the Greeks, where failure to observe and act accordingly

---

[1] Note, for example, how Thucydides presents the Melian Dialogue in 'the History of the Peloponnesian War'.

draws down the severest correction. The contemporary need, in ancient times, lies dormant. Contemporary human beings, by comparison, strive to find out who they are, each in his or her own way, and they do not mind drawing the rest of creation empathetically into their search. In this way they recreate the modern world, both for themselves and for others.

Modern man chooses to stand halfway between the ancients and contemporary men and women. He is mythical and must forever vacillate between the two. His desire to unite the two is his wish to become contemporary and real. Finding out what he is can therefore not satisfy him but it should be the beginning of the search for who he is. For the ancients 'know yourself', if we take into account what they mean by knowing, is a life-serving practice and the idea is that while they know this, they fare well. Accidents can therefore be explained in terms of insufficient effort and success in terms of such knowledge.

For modern man, knowledge and knowing what one amounts to is always a somewhat fearful undertaking, 'in case one finds out'. The possibility of a final, all-revealing knowledge, is therefore obscured in the mythical realm of an afterlife and any amount of magic is employed for the purpose of self-deception, not to mention the deception of others. Of course the fact that magic is not recognizable as such, except from the point of view of contemporary spirit, does not help matters.

The modern search for the modern salvation remains fearful, though hopeful at the same time. For two millennia this fearful/hopeful search has continued, always intense and desperate, always intolerant of the heretic, who says he knows what he amounts to, thereby threatening the official tradition and orthodoxy of the modern mind-set.

I agree with Albert Schweitzer's conclusion that most of the sayings of Jesus of Nazareth contain an eschatological kernel, a sense of comparison between now and later, between here and afterwards. So for instance the saying I quoted earlier neatly by-passes the modern dilemma and would teach us to pass straight from ancient into contemporary being. For the ancients, who would know themselves, the only fear that mattered was the one for the safety of the body. For contemporary men and women however, a soul and consequently danger to the soul becomes relevant. The knowledge of, or rather the knowing of, who I am automatically encompasses this new fear, so that the journey, or transformation, from ancient to contemporary, which was the one of especial interest to Jesus, should encompass also a knowledge of this new fear, which made the old one unnecessary and irrelevant. With contemporary reality in your sights, he says, fear the one who would harm your soul by way of your body, not the one who knows only of our body. Do this and no modern problems will arise. No myths or magic will occur to you as in any way helpful. The reason for the fear of the one who can harm our body was to preserve our body. The reason for the fear of the one who harms body and soul is the preservation of body and soul. The former fear is no longer of use once we have set out on the path to contemporary reality. For the ancients, contemporary reality did not yet lie within the realm of possibilities. Nowadays it is almost impossible to continue to be ancient for any appreciable period of time since the door to contemporary life is wide open and *those who do not seek to go in are progressively unnerved by what comes out.*

*

Creative spirit would, among other things, persuade us to grow. It's up to us whether we actually do grow. We can acquire habits of growth but also habits of decay. Let each decide what is best for him or her in terms of growth. Nothing you can point to is bound to be good or bad for everyone. I myself, for example, realize I must not be too hard on myself but more circumspect, often leisurely, sometimes a little crazy and aware for as long as possible. I can do with a moderate amount of sleep but I must have it regularly. I aim for eight hours because I realize I need to regulate this pattern, while all the same staying ready for extraordinary calls on my time, when I can go quite long without sleep. I do well always to keep my pen on the go, even if it's only a sketch or a notation for later use. Once I have started on a larger work I try to continue with it a little every day. However if circumstances disallow, I do not argue with this, for I try always to keep in mind that as for the time and the timing, there is one who judges better than I. He lets me know in good time if I should change my behaviour and if he finds me unsure as to whether to abide or not, he gently repeats his request several times and sets me an example of patience until I chance upon the fitting way. I used to enjoy a lot of energetic walking and climbing but when I began to practice my vocation I took no more time for that but devoted every minute, under the most diverse circumstances, to the practicing of my craft. When the time came to raise a family and to make a home, I learned the rudiments of carpentry and of building in stone until our house was decently in shape and furnished. I turned wood on a lathe for a while. Then I learned to compose for the piano and gained much pleasure from that. I try to keep up a few pieces of music, so that when desire moves me I can play a Chopin Nocturne, some Mozart or perhaps one of my own pieces. These latter are mostly atonal. For a time tonality disgusted me. The aleatory experience mattered. Then I am perfectly content playing familiar classical pieces again for a while.

While we raised our children, little time was left for anything else. Even our enjoyments and pleasures were child-centred. Looking back, I sometimes wish that at times I had behaved diferently. I feel I over-controlled our children's behaviour and especially now, when I take so much delight in spending parental time with my grandchildren, I wish I had adopted a more leisurely approach with my own children. I reacted to the fashion of the time, which judged that children did not need to be brought up, since one had no notion what that was in any case. The idea was to pawn them off on some institution as early as possible, I mean such as a school, a church or girl guides and boy scouts and the like. I sent our youngest child to a non-institutional school, where individual teachers were themselves responsible, and I have never regretted that. That boy turned out more confident, less concerned about mere appearances and fashionable behaviour. Anyone would have employed him when the time came, even though he had spent only the minimum number of years at school and had not gone in for any specialist training. Now my daughter 'home-schools' her own children. It will be a few decades yet before we human beings learn that institutional schooling is not much good for our children, but I don't want to get technical here. I was the first in Northern Ireland to take the law by its word. I said we could educate them perfectly well if not better at home. However in those days they were, as a consequence, short of playfellows. Nowadays my grandchildren have friends who come from families that 'home-school'. I never say we should get rid of schools. I make no political statements. For the great majority, and also for those who have no family life, institutionalized schooling will be the only choice for who can say how long, while alternative ways of learning for the young will multiply. (In some so-called underdeveloped countries, schools become crucial because they supply a much needed upbringing.) Those who are responsible for law and public order must of course remain vigilant but for aware human beings those restraints are barely necessary. Upbringing at home, parental care and attention from the ever more extended community, brings a child to maturity. An acquaintance of mine is sixty. He was ignored at school. He can neither read nor write but his instinctive and intuitive nature has developed very happily. He feels he might learn to read and write even now but he sees no need for it. He is never out of work very long and he enjoys what he does and this is attractive for those who employ him.

*

We are human naturally urged to grow and we do well, as adults, to co-operate with that urgency. It is entirely up to me that I speak of creative spirit as agent of

22

that urgency. At times I prefer to speak of 'the' creative spirit because not only do I feel physically influenced but also personally addressed. To whom would I apologize for not appealing to popular opinion? To philosophers? To scholars? To critics?

I speak to those who feel similarly urged and who would like to make sense, or more sense, of something that seems at times to bewilder them and at other times to expose them to censure. What I am suggesting is that they can think and feel, i.e. know, in such a way that this urge, this drive, this stimulus, will reveal to them its true nature and that this nature will turn out to be human; and being human, that it serves human beings marvellously well.

Really we human beings are not in the least concerned whether anyone morally or intellectually 'higher' is pleased with us and sanctions our behaviour. We do not even suppose we should feel constrained to explain to anyone why we know and experience as we do or to justify our being and doing to any higher authority. Is it arrogant of me to say 'we human beings'? I know that it is not, but if that is your opinion I will not argue with you. I have spent a lot of time knowing and understanding what being and human being is, what human nature is, what a human being is and I shall continue to know and to say it, to understand and to speak it.

How unseemly for human beings to become involved in arguments and disputes about politics or religion! How absurd for us to concern ourselves about nationality or social justice! People can do this much more effectively. Disrespect for people harms us. Let us honour the honest disposition and the decent behaviour wherever we find it.

Let your intentions towards people be respectful. Coming from a human being, respect is nothing to be scoffed at. People know how to value and appreciate it, especially on account of its unconditional nature. They sense they do not have to earn it or to defend themselves against its opposite and as a consequence they do not mind seeming human for a time, which certainly makes things easier for us human beings.

It makes no sense for us to preach honesty and decency to people. What our intention and behaviour does not show them, our words cannot teach them. Meanwhile let those to whom it is given to do so preach humanity to human beings, so that we may become more aware of ourselves and more insightful within our nature.

Happy among happy people we tend to forget who we are. Happiness does not become us. Whatever happens to us is raw and in need of refinement. For that we need strong nerves. First the identification, then the treatment. Let us be prepared for an ongoing adjudication. We can practice being glad beyond our pain threshold. Then, when the time is ripe, our joy exceeds all expectation.

Shall we hold it against people that they do not know us? On no account. What would they be if they did? Not people but human beings. Is the credit ours for being human? Not at all. When we make mistakes we wish we had done better and that is that. We know how to apologize. Are we afraid of being misunderstood? We have nothing against repeating ourselves, in many tongues, on several occasions, with a few alternatives in mind and always that one truthful intention.

Even we human beings do not always understand one another. In fact we seem to have an exceptional capacity for hurting one another. After all, ours is not only a wish for personification but at the same time a struggle for individuation. Mature growth encompasses both. Who we are and what we amount to changes from time to time. Why else would we learn? We cherish our capacity for learning.

*

Human beings do not think they are better than people. There is no point of comparison. In many ways people are more proficient than human beings. Some people are aware of the difference between themselves and human beings. They are like interpreters and we do well to value their services. So much depends on people and human beings not misunderstanding each other! They can benefit from each other. Harm is done by those who seek a common denominator, such as a morality or an ethic, that will benefit both. A popular morality can be permitted to work out itself. There is no need for a 'holy man' to get mixed up in it. He will only make them self-conscious and unhappy as a result. People have their own way of dealing with the particular circumstances of their locality and with the changing demands made on them by their environment. Popular artists have their role to play and should not be made to feel uneasy by those who demand universal virtues or values. When people are left alone by misguided intellectuals and ambitious theologians they develop a folk morality simply based on their healthy instinct for survival. Culture regains its meaning as the express identity of a popular community.

Many of the distressing phenomena of the modern world fall away when finally people and human beings no longer confuse humanity and popularity. Let it be a case of 'to each his own'. This is the first step. What can be contemplated then is mutual assistance. However there is some way to go until then.

Organized religion is probably the most typical symptom of confusion between humanity and popularity. No one can truly benefit from it. It deceives on one side and outrages on the other. Human beings cannot be satisfied by it and people are unnecessarily burdened in a way that disallows them their characteristic development as folk communities, where each contributes his or her instinctive talent for survival, always of benefit to many.

Popular religion is love of god and neighbour. What need is there for organisation or committee decisions, for a governing body? Let people rid themselves as gently as possible from such encumbrances. Let them look into themselves and decide whether they would not be better off with the practices and rituals they unconsciously invent for themselves, uninfluenced by the 'holy men'.

It is the so-called 'Holy Men' who legislate for all. There is only one way of making fish and fowl appear the same and that is by destroying the characteristics of both. Surely human beings understand people sufficiently to help them realize their potential – as people. And surely people have sufficient regard for human beings to honour them as different. The great egotistic legislators make it a source of pride that they have 'come for all' and therefore 'all' must be explained alike and squeezed into a procrustean bed of intellectual conformity. Even the Jesus of the Jews came, as he purportedly stated, for a select group, probably for 'the remnant', but soon after his death his message was accommodated as suitable for all, in the name of orthodoxy and organization. Soon it becomes apparent that those who profess to know him well enough for all really know him least, as their passion for individualistic control gets the better of them; as they trim and twist to accommodate what they misperceive to their notion of popular success.

The 'holy men', as I call them, are therefore not holy at all but their souls are twisted by the contraction – as they see it – of popular and human.

Let those with the gift for humanity limit their resources as they work on behalf of human beings, benefiting a few, several or many. Let them altogether eschew popularity, as a claim to fame or as a guarantee of credibility. Let them come out from among people so that eventually they may return as whole human beings. Meanwhile let people become honourable by honouring.

*

This is really what modernity was about, and what it is still about, namely this extraction of the human from the popular. However in the absence of some reflection we have a thoroughly misleading statement on our hands here. After all, neither the human nor the poplar existed as such, prior to that mysterious extraction, to which frequent and mysterious reference is made throughout the ages by those who could not help themselves but they had to mention it, no other way lay open for arriving at an explanation of apparently irreconcilable differences and downright contradictory points of view. How indeed was one to account for absolutely certain experiences of a mystical, of a divine, nature side by side with honest conviction of life centred finitely in finite matter? This had nothing to do with schools of thought but went much deeper, as witness the readiness to torture and burn those who still dared to work against the committee-orthodoxy of a few souls who were equally persuaded of their rightness, of their just cause, and of the need to stamp out all opposition, if their supposed humanity was to survive. And this not exclusively in the realm of religion and politics but equally in the home and household, in the very heart and soul of caring individuals. By no means was this a straightforward struggle.

Words that have been and are still used to stir the disturbed melting pot are 'mankind', 'the human race', or even 'man'. Upon these the provocative and evocative pronouncements are made that cannot but give birth to party spirit, to schism and denomination, to race hatred and class struggle, indeed to the animosity between brother and brother, mother and daughter, father and son. 'If only we knew why this strife is necessary', so went the outcry of a few, always a few, caring individuals, as they spent their life's blood speculating, inventing, sacrificing in the performance of seemingly thankless tasks under the cold stare of historical judgment.

A little was always gained. Always a little. Would a time come when all these mites, added up, would permit a retrospective glance that would reveal the final, all-excusing purpose? A time when all would be forgiven, the atrocities, the small-mindedness, the unthinking, unseeing, unfeeling reaction to reaction and again to reaction?

It is not only possible but even likely that the names of those who really and truly knew what they were doing – I mean in the light of the overall purpose – are historically unknown and will remain so. It was always in their interest, and in the interest of the goal they pursued, to remain anonymous. Certainly progress was made, in the home, in the lecture hall, invisibly on the battle front, wherever someone experienced in his soul the love of enemy, the growth in spirit, the reason for pain and he or she acted accordingly. We might liken it to the drop by drop accumulation of heart-wisdom as pain is intelligently suffered, however on a cosmic scale, until the atoll rises out of the sea and universal vision is born. Judgment ceases. All along, final judgment took its course. Whatever happened to us and whatever we did was ruled in the name of this constellation called final judgment. Even those, perhaps especially those, who saw fit to push the final judgment into an unknown future, did their bit in the name of that very judgment. Call it final because beyond it there is no more judgment, because the human race, mankind – man – has been judged.

*

Child of god, child of spirit,

Both of these I am and do.

Never speak to me of merit

Lest you mention mercy too.

*

Let those who disparage popularity be informed of their shortcoming. When I pick up a popular book, I am overcome, after reading the first few paragraphs, by a type of nausea. Quickly I lay it down again. If I were to subject that book to a critique I would first have to overcome that nausea, which would not be so difficult if I were to put my mind to it. All the same, my mind would ask me: Should I turn against myself? Surely that could not be in your best interest. I have informed you of a limit, a limit both natural and spiritual. Heed those limits. Remain within your sphere and prosper. Step out of it and incur needless pain, unprofitable insofar as it can only teach you what you well know by now. Men, women and children live in community. People, by comparison are social beings. Has it not taken nearly a lifetime for us to withdraw the human from the popular, thereby coincidentally liberating the popular from the would-be human?

Yes, if people are left in peace to sort out their affairs and human beings remain unencumbered by considerations of popularity, world will rejoice. Add only to this that human beings respect people and that people honour human beings and you finally have a recipe for 'the family of man'. The occasion of it is cause for celebration.

What have we had until now? We have had the modern world. The family of man has been a distant ideal on the horizon. Potential human beings and dissatisfied people have interacted, have made both reasonable and unreasonable efforts to co-exist, while the family of man, as idea and ideal, as profession and prophecy, has advanced step by little step, while this true progress, physical and spiritual at once, has never been honestly noted or correctly defined. It might not be an entirely unrewarding pastime for once to view the two millennia of modern striving – at once stubbornly conservative and optimistically revolutionary – historically in the light of the family of man. I see it as more to the point however that both people and human beings increasingly learn to view themselves in this light.

At this early date I would consider it advisable to speak of mandatory respect and voluntary honour. On one hand, people, to 'get it right', will learn to distinguish between, on one hand, the honourable approach and attitude to human beings and on the other hand, all types of slavishness and resentment. Human beings, meanwhile, in the interest of their true human nature, will learn to discern the spirit of respectfulness as quite discrete from contempt and affection.

Is it not almost as if human beings and people were two species? In much they are similar but in what are they the same? Indeed, now that we come to the point, can we put our finger on a common denominator? I sincerely believe that to do so would be to falsify the matter in hand. Human beings grow. They wait for the time to be ripe – for whatever. Their being and doing is growth-oriented. They will not be rushed or delayed. They learn and are taught this value of growth-related time and of time-related growth early in their lives. The sense for the right time is bred into them. Let each take delight in his enlightened possession of that sense – which can be diminished, distorted, exalted. What better source of my identity in comparison to yours! Does such-and-such work for you?

No. decidedly not. Or at least not yet. Ah, now it does. And for you? Not any longer? In that case ... etc.

Human beings get to know one another. There is little to go by at first, except perhaps a degree of animosity, for let's face it, your being impinges upon mine, as surely as mine does upon yours. There is opportunity here, finally even need, for accommodation. We grow at different rates, have arrived at different points, feel urged in different directions. And yet we do well to take seriously, not excluding merriment, the occasion of our meeting, in short, the syncreticity of our being.

People do not grow. They are now as they were and as they shall be. They differ from one another in terms of character and mood. What matters is that their existence coincides with ritual, rite and remembrance. For this coincidence their consciousness is refined to a point. Instead of growth there is co-existence – on several levels of choice perhaps but co-existence all the same. Remembrance dictates the march of time in a forward direction. Ritual spurs and arrests. Rite freshens up. As a result people exist moderately, neither at risk nor ever at their wits' end.

*

As human beings come out from among people, voluntarily, people come onto themselves, coincidentally. People sometimes try to get rid of human beings from among themselves, however in this they are misguided, in that they try to do themselves what has to be done for them. All the same the popular integrity cannot confine itself simply to waiting. That is one predicament. Not being able to wait, they say: We are bound to make a few bad moves. Bad indeed.

The popular badness is unavoidable. What if human beings had not understood this? Would they have heaped the consequences for avoidable evil-doing upon their heads? And so indeed many of them did. Woe on one side, worse on the other. We can hardly compare the 'wages of sin' to unavoidable errors. Badness and evil. The modern sorting process. Progress towards contemporary existence and life. The simple failure of the potential human being to recognize the necessary plurality of people attracts 'hellfire'.

Some of my comments are bound to appear veiled. Into whose hands will these pages fall? Even though an image of the true and real 'final solution' now exists, how will this change the appearance of things? In another sense, I do write down what I experience and see, though of course I learn to see better daily as my own identity is increasingly confirmed and as I behave in accordance with what I daily learn. The overall trend is unmistakable. Both tendencies, the popular and the human, are being documented. In the end neither trend nor tendency holds.

Not two species then either. The new language still has to be learned. Accustomed as we are to categorical judgments and critical evaluations, the way forward is bound to be one of disruption and humility. Non-acceptance of the final judgment disfigures and leads to removal from the scene. Full acceptance implies speedy recovery, health and well-being.

*

Now we need to ask: How do human beings restore, maintain and confirm one another's humanity?

First, what is to be avoided here, if not that sudden collapse of character that brings human beings themselves into disrepute! Very likely the cause is self-forgetfulness and – I think this has to be said – a shunning of people. I would not go so far as to suggest that human nature must ever lean on the popular. That would be contrary to it. No, but turning away from the popular, once this is no longer of the essence, no longer to the point, this must always have the effect of a self-defeating gesture. We shall not do it if we can at all help it. Respect for the popular, even for popularity, cannot harm us, while ignorance or disrespect of it is ever a set-back. However we still need to ask how we may keep this ability of respect alive, this respectability, as a skill; how to keep it from turning into mere form, empty observancy. Not grudging, ironic, but actual, heart-felt respect is required, bordering on affection, patently devoid of contempt. Practice alone, as towards a good habit, cannot entirely serve us, for what matters is not what we do but who and how we are. In other words we, as human beings, cannot consistently respect the people near us unless we are personal and strong human beings, rooted in humanity and growing human-naturally. How we can manage that we will eventually discover, for it depends on how we behave towards one another, human being to human being.

Self-forgetfulness and the shunning of people go hand in hand. Keep in mind that there are so many more people than human beings. The human being who loses awareness of him- or herself as a growing and creative person needs to be made aware of this as soon as possible and it seems that the popular element is very well suited to remind him or her. How? You could not count the ways. You could not guard against it on account of those infinite possibilities. You could not possibly ensconce yourself humanistically for very long before the popular flood would pour through your dyke. Did you think human perfection would allow for the death of form?

All these truths are played out now on a personal level. Social movements, revolutions, cultural ideals are no longer to the point. The history of ideas need no longer concern us. Nationalism, communism, capitalism are anachronistic side-shows. Religions, pedagogic trends, civilization as such can no longer hold our interest. All these are modern phenomena and those who insist on them as relevant to mental or physical development, not to mention the status of their soul, are out on a limb that cracks under their weight. Psychologically they are skating on thin ice, not so much because of what they know and do but on account of what they refrain from doing and neglect to do. Only where our individual/personal reality each and every time comes into its own, that is where the last judgment bears fruit.

On what, then, does awareness of ourselves depend? Surely we would not expect to have to walk around practicing some individual virtue! Our delivery from sin resides in the communal realm. Sin is betrayal of the communal realm. The question we need to ask therefore is: What is the substantial and sustaining element of human community? What we are looking for is equally at home in us and capable of being created by us. This is especially important and we might reflect upon it a bit. As human beings we live in community and behave communally. Creatively we build community. Living communally, we exemplify human being.

The love we human-naturally bear for one another is merciful and reverential. Let us further reflect on what this means. Morality cannot help us because we cannot depend on obeyed rules and regulations. Not since we know who we are can we depend on that. At the same time we sustain pain periodically. I think of it as growth-stimulus. By being careful we will minimize this pain. Being careful means loving mercifully and reverentially as much as possible. Nonetheless some growth-stimulus, some pain of that sort, comes our way. Someone called it the salt that assures our savour. We suffer it as best we can. We do not always understand it right away and so we react. That aggravates the pain, perhaps only a little, before we love mercifully and reverentially.

Keep in mind that it is the same love. Directed towards people it turns out mercifully; shared with other human beings it is reverential.

Why do I write this down? What do I promise myself? When all is said and done, this is my way of learning. It is also my way of caring for others. I don't get paid for it, moreover it is my main satisfaction in life, which makes it possible for me not to be dissatisfied with anyone else. People in my presence sometimes get nervous, fidgety. Then I raise my respect level. Not that they ever pick on me. At times I am quite glad to have some of them around. How disrespectful that sounds! I must watch myself more carefully. When suddenly a human being turns up, things become lively. We feel each other out, looking for profit and benefit. It's all about life and a greater abundance of it.

People do not have this craving for life. They are perfectly content if they are allowed to exist after a manner. Their struggle for existence has to do with surviving as long as possible and often their existence surpasses in riches the existence of human beings nearby. Then the human being, to avoid envy or disappointment, reminds himself that there is richness of existence and a wealth of life and since the latter is for him he withdraws from the former. This act of withdrawal is sometimes necessary as he confirms his penchant for life, which after all does include existence. If he gets caught up in a struggle for a more colourful existence he is eventually urged out of this by despair and a sense of loss. He interprets this correctly as a merciful corrective and expresses his gratitude. It is not up to him now to belittle and criticize popular existence. He is saved from this by confirming his enjoyment of life.

We can see how much native understanding is in play here. What people sense of human life stimulates in them an honourable disposition. They value this highly and naturally associate it with human personality, as they come across it.

An honourable disposition is the high point of popular existence. It would never occur to people to strive for this, except by honouring human life wherever they come across it. They do not have to train or school themselves in this, for they arrive at it existentially, by virtue of their existence. In other words, as people strive for existence, they enable within themselves an honourable disposition. It comes about organically, as a result of their work, which is not creative but cumulative. They do not overcome, by their work, hindrances to life for the sake of more and more abundant life but they accumulate capacities, abilities, skills for existing for a longer period of time.

This allows us now to distinguish between popular and human art. It is the talented popular artist's task and responsibility to facilitate survival by making available lively and enlivening entertainments. The human artworker is endowed with genius, which means he is able to show human life in all its splendour. The difference between talent and genius is the same as that between popular and human, between artist and art-worker.

There is no such thing as 'a' genius in reality; that is a modern conception, which testifies to a lack of understanding of the difference between human and popular.

The human art worker creates eventualities. We will understand this better if we put modern art out of our mind for the moment. One element is the prophetic. Present times are compared to past times and a projection is made. Then there is the historic element. Present time is used as a milestone which allows for a construction of past time. Also there is the contemporary element, which allows for the art-worker's remembered experience to be made memorable. And last but not least there is the humorous and playful element, the function of which is the levity that enlightens human existence.

These are the four elements of creative art-work. We can see to what extent the perception of time, the time and the times is involved and relevant. Once an art-worker has begun, he believes that his work will eventually come true. This faith in the meaningfulness of creativity is crucial. Every hindrance overcome leaves room for a new creation. This is also why art-work at times is extremely difficult. The extremity of present conditioning has to be explored inasmuch as the art-worker's mind, body and soul are conditioned by present circumstances. Much as the art-worker prefers to depict contemporary reality, his sense of mission prevents him from ignoring present and past time. He knows he is inwardly accountable for confronting things as they are and accepting beings as they might be. He bears within his soul, as it were, the watermark of human perfection.

*

This separation of the human from the popular, which has been going on over the past two millennia, ever since that certain sword was introduced into the world, can from now on be experienced as a fact. It is complete insofar as cosmic reality is concerned. In other words, what will be relevant for discussion from now on is not the more or less esoteric progress towards that goal but the nature of the goal achieved, by those who are more or less informed.

The goats give milk, the sheep give wool – if that ancient metaphor of the goats and the sheep should still be acceptable. Both the external and internal turmoil of mankind, the agonies and ecstasies of individuals and nations, the struggles on behalf of faith or reason, con-

39

servative or liberal, religion or worldly enlightenment, can now be understood sympathetically as symptomatic manifestations of the one thing necessary, namely the inexorable process towards popular and human being, both in themselves.

More than ever does one now have to be careful how one speaks of these phenomena. Those who cannot distinguish between the times and the time had better speak of something else. The time is that of a human life in readiness. The time presents advantages unimaginable until then. It contains riches ultimately both fascinating and rewarding. The times, on the other hand, are of this or of that, of fleeting interest, perhaps as raw material for him who knows how to shape and escape them. The times will never surprise us, for we who select them, for whatever reason, nevertheless have good and predicable reason for selecting just them. While the time is organic, the times are photographic.

The here and now is humanly real while time present and time past lends the popular experiment its charm. What artist does not rub his hands in glee for a chance to manage a conjunction of the two, such as when some discovered aspect of his environment merges with a memory or two. The highly questionable impulse that ties him to those times is laid to rest as soon as he produces some static, repeatable representation. His mission is popular, therefore his aim is limited to the realm of the moral. Within that limitation – let it be said emphatically – countless possibilities for colourful treatment, hence for lively and enlivening entertainment, present themselves.

The here and now, by comparison, is the art worker's domain. Here he reaps what the spirit of the ages has sown. Let him comply with that spirit in every way possible. Not morality but ethics pertains to his creative activity, not as a limitation but rather as a duty. With bewildering ambiguity his inventiveness is tested, while his initiative, foreordained to the creative principle, is free to exert itself on behalf of whatever reveals itself to him as presentable and noteworthy. Understand that his experiential personification of the ethical domain is total. He cannot but move and be moved therein. His personal freedom lies precisely in his submission, unfortunately begrudging or joyfully selfless, to both novel and time-tried recipes for immortality and eternal life.

*

Since humanity is the essence of being, which implies that all that is is human, we need to realize that people are human too. The distinguishing mark of human beings however resides in the fact that not only are they human because they are, essentially human, but they are, in addition, human by attribute, existentially. Not only are they human but they also 'do' human.

The fact that human beings are ethical removes them from all other beings in terms of a common existence and returns them to those beings on the basis of merciful and reverential love. In other words, when I, as a human being, experience some natural occurrence, this experience, if you can call it that, leaves me open to doubt as to the reality of what I have experienced. I experience this doubting the same was as I experienced the primal reality, prior to any voluntary creative response on my part.

Along with the appearance comes the doubt that this may last, however at the same time I have the confidence that it lies in my hands to bear the responsibility for this mere, this primal, ideal reality and that within me resides the power for reparation, for making good. Very little time, if any, do I spend indulging my senses in the idol which only exists due to my partial vision, initially liable. What foolishness now to dwell on the error, albeit comparative error, of the less than up-to-date judgment! Finally I know – and understand – how the halfway, modern experience and the ethically powerful behaviour go hand in hand as true and lively growth-orientation; the good deed makes good both the introductory experience, comparatively faulty, and any dwelling-upon, for whatever reason, on faulty vision's result. Merciful love deals with incurred guilt while reverential love welcomes reality in truth, trusts the new dispensation, clears the path for what growth encounters.

I would make final judgment acceptable. I would discourage any further dwelling on mere appearance, call it romantic or whatever. I would show how ethical behaviour is human-naturally growth-responsive and growth-creative. Both actively and passively do we grow. We are justified by both faith and good deed, inseparably.

The freedom to grow human-naturally may be hard won but thereafter it is easy to sustain. Take care not to get bogged down by specific issues, by this way or that way of saying or doing the same thing, for all things have come true and this is up to human beings to demonstrate, for one another and for all beings, a little at a time. Let there be no Philistine attachment to mental rigours or private doctrines. Let us gradually phase out our love-affair with magical beauty, our deplorable addiction to popular values if human nature is our lot. Let people take care of what is theirs. There is good reason why we have our skills and they have theirs. The road lies open to both people and human beings for respectful and honourable co-operation. There is no more need for aristocracy and slavery, for rebellion and revolution.

*

Ideal beauty, magical beauty – our nerves seem to be habituated to it: a deplorable state of affairs. The primal reality is not the finished product. How regrettable that so much time has been invested, over the years, again and again, in attempts to perpetuate ideal beauty! Idolatry of beauty causes nerve-decay. In human beings, that is. People are not troubled by it. Why not? Because primal reality is properly their bread and butter. Caesar deals in primal reality. Why are human beings so unhappy with primal reality? Why does the existential doubt set in, the doubt of which people know nothing? Simply because that is what human being is about. The difference between essential and existential does not occur to people, or at least not with the same meaning. Human beings initially are in sympathy with the essence of a thing, whereupon they are painfully stimulated to contribute an ethical existence, with the result that that which was essentially perceived as a thing is subsequently known as a being, perhaps even a human being. People take things as they come and arrive at moral arrangements and compromises. A distinction between things and beings is not open to them. In fairness therefore one would have to say

43

that they take what comes as it comes. When they speak of 'things' they cannot possibly mean what human beings mean by that word. Immense confusion has arisen out of this indiscriminate use of 'popular being' and human being. Since I look at people from the point of human being I can well enough tell if something is popular and not human but it would be dishonest of me to arrive at a value judgment of poplar being or of the popular soul. With all due respect I can make allowances for what is not available to my perception but it would not do for me to criticize or to demean. Even an ironic approach to the popular world is dishonest, because I do not live in that world, having thrown in my lot with infinite human world and those who know it.

*

Any serious attempt to portray ideal beauty is surely a betrayal of human being, inasmuch as the ethical creation that is possible is short-circuited and short-changed. The situation is worsened if this ideal beauty is presented in a moral light. Ideal beauty is a human perception, vouchsafed to potentially human beings, so that they will ethically actuate their perception. If potentially human beings turn heir backs on ethical creation in an attempt to appeal to the popular world, this is both disrespectful to people and dishonourable to human beings.

The emphasis is on human beings treating people respectfully, not on trying to persuade them to treat human beings honourably. Nothing puts paid to he respect more readily than thinking that 'after all they are only people'. This 'only' shows an assumption that people do not come up to scratch in terms of human being, which is totally wrong because, as we must never tire of reminding ourselves and one another, human beings and people have nothing in common that might be indulged or achieved more by human beings than by people, or the other way around. After all there are those who are neither human beings nor people and they do deserve our contempt. Our respect for them meets with blatant disrespect. Our contempt leaves them with no response whatsoever and thereafter we have nothing to do with them. We call them the nameless ones and their number is legion.

*

What we call growth in the case of a human being implies an openness to change and a willingness to respond to that change creatively. Much of a human being's daily attentiveness is taken up by the registration, interpretation and recreation of inward and outward change.

Inwardly there is the change of mood and disposition, of humour and temperament. Even our constitution is suddenly liable to be affected by spirit of one sort or another. This inwardness is our essential being and we begin our creative living from within, where the scene is never the same from one day to the next, so that we can justly say that each day brings the problems sufficient onto it. Our attitude towards what we encounter within ourselves is preferably one of discerning and cheerful acceptance.

At the same time – and why not at the same time? – we experience reality from without. The sun shines upon us, birds twitter and a breeze ruffles the leaves and sways

45

the long grass. This is where our creativity comes into its own, for the outward and the inward reality cannot coincide except in our soul, where the two, so to speak, marry. Much however may stand in the way of this marriage. For example, we are not always persuaded that we find ourselves in the right place at the right time. So we quarrel with the outward reality and neglect the inward. Conversely we may disagree with the inward and ignore the outward. As a result a variety of dissonances accumulate. Dissension arises between spirits from without and spirits from within. We get caught up in this and miss the centre of our being. How fortunate that we are capable of merciful and reverential love! We have practiced it often enough, so there is no reason why it should not come to our aid at this moment of need. We do it now, this love, and overcome the dissonance, the disagreement and whatever else prevents our soul, which is to say 'us', from living a cheerful life. Naturally the mix of outward and inward reality is never twice the same and this makes for the richness of our life, for its luxury and abundance. Another word for this creative love in action is worship. We worship, we human beings, in reality and in truth, outwardly and inwardly.

* *

So this is what we have come up with by studying that particular instance, or experience, of nervous being. We can look at the results now and we can decide what we want to do with them. Would anyone be able to benefit from our findings? Perhaps.

* * *

(2009)

2
A Few Related Concepts
pertaining to the philosophic description
of human beings as such

At the age of sixty-six I am an adult, male human being, more or less mature much of the time. I was an infant at one time, then a child, then I grew through adolescence to adulthood. During that time I was young. I don't ever intend to be old, but that may happen now and again.

I intend, here, to present a few concepts as I commonly use them. All of them hinge upon the way human beings can be described. By beginning with these concepts and then gradually embedding them in meaningful usage as I personally see it I hope to cast light, once again and in yet another fashion, on a topic that has never ceased to interest me, which is human beings seen from within and from without.

One way of relating what we mean specifically by certain given concepts is by applying them descriptively or expressively during the course of narrative. So for example you would get   some notion of what I mean by the term 'homeland' if you took note of how I use the word in the course of a memoir. In this present tract I intend to go about it the other way around, by starting with the word and then building specific meaning around it – always as I personally see it. I make no claim to universality of meaning nor, on the other hand, do I admit the constraints of any particular academic discipline. I intend the account to be personally definitive.

*

I begin with the concepts to which all the others pertain, namely **'human being'**, **'a human being'** and **'the human being'**. All three will lead us, upon scrutiny, to their own particular terrains and provinces of meaning. As I pursue this course of action I draw on a store of knowledge that does not fit in with any school or tradition of thought but it is a part of what I have accumulated during a life dedicated to original thought and creativity. I would not wish anyone to suppose that I mean solely my own original thought but original thought wherever I have come across it and cherished it. I honestly feel that if we can distinguish between what we have gained from others and what we have come up with ourselves we must have something other than original thought in mind, because original thought is such that it does not allow exclusive borders to be erected around its perimeter. The same original thought, however, can be related or communicated in one way or another, and that is where individual personality comes into its own.

Human being: When is being human? Under what circumstances would I refer to 'my' human being? When is my being human rather than otherwise? These are questions that deserve an answer and such answers will presuppose at least an acquaintance with being as such. In other words, in agreement with Shakespeare's Hamlet, I can choose to be or not to be. Or let's put it this way: I can choose to be, and frequently I am even though I have not specifically chosen to do so, but technically non-being presupposes an absence of choice. By saying 'chosen to do so' I imply that being is a kind of doing, and this is quite correct, inasmuch as we admit that doing does not necessarily bring along with it material consequences. To contemplate, to relate, to run and jump, to fix the plumbing – these are all kinds of doing inasmuch as they involve the consent of the one who does. In the same way, when I decide to be, simply to be, I am actively and passively around, on earth and in the world. I can be without necessarily being happy or sad, here or there. The fact that simply being means that action and passion are not yet distinct is perhaps a telling qualification for being and we might do well to keep it in mind for the time being.

It is not until we understand that being is recognizable by the one who is, that we can have a worthwhile notion of human being. **He who knows that he is, when he is, is human.** Now just as there are degrees of knowledge, from mere consciousness to awareness, from supposition to certainty, from merely knowing to perfect understanding, there must also, therefore, be degrees of human being. Nonetheless what we mean when we say that 'humanity is the essence of being' is that we are owning up to the fact that nothing can in any real and down to earth sense be said to be unless a human being perceives it or is aware of it, and it is this implied recognition that allows us to make genuine good sense of the fact that something is. What point would there be in our saying that we know that something is, if that something were to lie somehow outside or beyond our humanity? You might say that our humanity confers knowability on that which therefore is. It would be as silly to ask: What is it before we know it? as to ask: What existed prior to time. Modesty forbids.

A human being: It might clarify things if we remind ourselves that that which is, as a being, is not necessarily a human being. Human beings are beings that are able to know other beings; not things, now, but beings. Things are beings the humanity of which is being ignored. They are at best potential beings. So for a being to be a human being 'it' must become, philosophically, a 'he' or a 'she' due to this understanding and recognition of him- or herself as living at the very centre of universal creation where humanity is the gift which may (or must) be passed on so that we may live in communion with many beings, human or otherwise. Mere existence among things, by comparison, is not worthwhile; under such conditions even human beings are liable to turn into things.

A short answer to the question: When is my being human? would be: When I am as I was at the moment when I was born. That is the concept to start with then. When we come into the world, as human beings, (and how could it be otherwise?) we begin right away to extend our humanity to what we come up against. That is how we are, right at the beginning, gifted with humanity and therefore in favour of sharing that gift, with whatever meets and greets us. The humanity is not only a gift but also a process of knowing and then recognizing. The knowing is of that which is our being as endowed with essential humanity. Right away therefore humanity is the essence of being. It is the essence of the beings we recognize as having been imbued by us with humanity. Prior to that, nothing is. Beyond that, nothing ever is. We may get sidetracked into talking as if there were something and we may stray into the dubious company of those who have decided in their hearts that there is no humanity but if that is the case, then we will hopefully soon be able and willing to return to how we were when we were born. Then we might well say we are 'born again'.

A child, even an infant, does not question that this is so but behaves in terms of it quite naturally. When we say that an infant is 'in favour' of passing on this gift of humanity we might also say that he readily cooperates with the tendency of this gift to be shared and that he is in no need of education before he is willing to 'give of himself'. This is what attracts us so wonderfully to the babe in the cradle. Thereafter of course a great deal depends on how he is brought up and what he is taught.

Being is always human and my being is human when I am as I was when I was born, namely gifted with the ability to know and therefore naturally sharing that gift with what, as a consequence, takes on being for me. Not only am I gifted with human being as soon as I am born, inasmuch as I bring human being into the world with me, ('trailing clouds of glory', as it were) but in addition to that I am a human being as soon as I respond to the light of day – in other words as soon as I open my eyes, or my ears; in still other words, as soon as I am in any way affected by what goes on around me. The short way of saying this is that the light of day (not daylight) awakens in me my sense of myself. Not of my self but of myself. There is a world of difference. We may have time to go into that later.

This sense of myself, this knowledge of myself, is of crucial importance because while my human being (my being human) naturally gives me an outward point of reference, my sense of myself is the inward one. While I have human being, the light of day enlightens me. It does so until and unless I put up barriers. Any materialistic or spiritualistic teaching, for instance, would be precisely such a barrier, because it misleads me into not responding to the light but reacting to the dark.

The human being: This is a mythic concept because it points to nothing in particular but it does draw our attention to something in a general way. It either presupposes foreknowledge of several particulars or is intended to influence us in favour of something against our better judgment. In the former case we call it an abstraction, in the latter case we do well to reject it as a myth. What is 'the human being' other than an agreed upon common denominator of several or even many human beings we have come across? It all depends on how and in what spirit we have come across them and what our reason is for wishing to pass on or to communicate such knowledge. Any agreement on myths is in any case dubious if not downright false. If I wish to endow something with mythic quality, perhaps for the purpose of drawing attention to the need for some particular behaviour in the light of things to come, (I mean rather than turning it, or allowing it to turn, into a myth), I will take care not to obliterate the real setting of what will, as a result of my endowment, be *a mythic being*. On the other hand I can only endow with mythic quality whatever lends itself to such treatment. *A myth*, by comparison, has neither mythic quality nor mythic character but only a magical appearance, which is liable to compromise our sense of reality. Those who hold in awe some particular myth are scandalized then by that which has the same name but possesses actual mythic quality and character. 'Are you the human being?' 'I am.' 'Crucify him!' – I can only give a short indication here of what I have treated at length elsewhere.

In conclusion, I am *human* inasmuch as I know that I am when I am and I am *a human being* when I share the gift of my knowledgeable humanity with others, either readily, like a newly born infant, or upon reconsideration, after having strayed into some form of selfishness.

*

Adulthood: Let us take a look now at what it might mean to be an adult. This is a concept that evidently has to do with development and growth. Biologically, when I am no longer a child I am an adult. The passage from childhood to adulthood is crucial and often critical.

We have to steer a careful course here around all the romanticized and sentimentalized aspects of these terms, not because we disparage romance and sentiment but because the underlying facts have to be clear first. We might say to someone: 'You are young at heart,' or: 'Will you never grow up!' but of course we are speaking affectionately or ironically.

Adulthood generally comes along between the ages of eighteen and twenty-five or so. What we need to take on board is that it comes along rather than being acquired, through education or training and that it is not a gift. After childhood and, hopefully, youthful childhood, comes adulthood. No one can predict exactly when because we all develop at a different rate. For those who hold themselves parentally responsible for the young, not only is it important to know what it means to be young compared to being adult but they would also wish to acquaint themselves with the peculiar human natural changes as youngsters not only grow up and are raised but also as they stop being children and become adult.

There are, for example, many kinds of parental approaches from which the young can benefit but these would be of no use if they were applied to an adult. An adult finds it unsuitable to be treated like a child and would be right to complain. Similarly it would be wrong to approach a child as though he were an adult because in that way that child's development would be neglected. What we have to do now is come to terms with some of the inward differences between adults and children, all of which are down to what is usually called 'natural development'.

Just as a child is not necessarily young, so is an adult not necessarily mature. (I say mature, not old.) A child can be so maltreated and mishandled that at the age of ten, say, there is nothing left of youth. In the same way and by the same token an adult may be so attached to childish ways that he is not mature. *This distinction between childhood and adulthood on one side and youth and maturity on the other is central to any appropriate understanding of a growing human being.*

So is it correct to say that after youth comes adulthood? It is, if we assume that children, up to the time when they are grown-up, are youthful. If only they were! Let's at least allow the following: In conception, childhood excludes maturity and adulthood excludes youth. Which does not prevent us from describing a mature adult as 'remarkably youthful' but what we should mean by that, I suppose, is that he or she is lively, exuberant, fresh in his approach to nature and the world, in other words he is and behaves in a way we commonly associate with all-around healthy children and not with disillusioned adults. When we think philosophically however we try to get the bare bones right. We are concerned with the foundation.

Sadly one sees children too who are no longer young. In view of this we may ask what, more specifically, it means to be young. From my own philosophical point of view it means that the youthful child is inwardly sound but not yet capable of outward direction. The inward soundness will have had to be conserved from birth and nourished by parental adults but outward direction is not a possibility until, so to speak, *the measure of childhood is complete.* Behaviour in terms of world environment is the province of adults, whether they do it well or not so well. The less mature adult does it not so well. Nonetheless all adults, mature or immature, are called upon and feel called upon to think and behave no longer solely in terms of inner urges and wishes but their *world environment lays claim to them and lays claims upon them.* (Instead of 'world environment' we might simply say 'world', avoiding 'the world', which, for better or worth, is a mythic concept.)

Since we are presently interested in adulthood, we should really take the closest possible look at this business of world-direction. By this I mean a more or less clearly perceived need to enter into exchanges with world-being.

Let's differentiate between a young child and a youthful child. Philosophically speaking, a young child would be a human being who is not yet an adult and whose youth has not been wasted, forfeited or betrayed. (I think we suspect by now what would be meant by an old child!) A youthful child, by comparison, would be a human being who is not yet, but just about, an adult and whose measure of youth is full. (We might keep in mind that however rarely we come upon this in reality, it is nonetheless a distinct possibility.)

The youthful child, then, in his or her innermost being, in other words as him- or herself, feels drawn towards 'world-being', (which includes communal being). In other words, he is drawn towards that which is foreign and strange and at the same time real and beautiful. Let's not get side-tracked by mere appearances here. A young person may feel more drawn to the rural than to the urban scene, more towards nature than towards art, even more towards community than to wider world-being but that which essentially does the attracting is *foreign and strange, and also real and beautiful.*

Just as we cannot cope intelligently with illness and sickness, with infirmity or perversity, unless we know what it means to be well, in the same way, if we are to help human beings through that crucial transition from childhood to adulthood, we must have some notion of the distinct possibility of an utterly unproblematic transition. Statistics do not enter into it. Of course one would wish that a youthful child, upon entering adulthood, right away knows him- or herself as mature but how often is that really the case? It is precisely the province of mature adults to concern themselves compassionately with the tragedies of unguided and misguided children and with the casualties of immature adults. At the same time they can only succeed in this to the extent of their own genuine maturity. An immature adult is of no use to anyone but must first look to his or her maturing growth, (which may well amount to a *fulfilling of the measure of his childhood*).

So when a youthful child first feels drawn to world and experiences an urge or a longing, in him- or herself, (the generic determination at this stage is crucial), to associate with world-being, which is *foreign and strange* but at the same time *real and beautiful*, what comes about in that young human being is what we might call a *within-realm*. The *inner being*, composed of dream, imagination and fantasy, and open to that child for refuge, for the exercise of developing faculties of muscle and will and also for spiritual sustenance, gradually turns into a *within-being*, or *within-ness*, readily available as *inward being*, while at the same time and at the same rate *outward being* is experienced and a certain curious *without-ness* plays into that human being's perception.

The available choice of *inward* or *outward* is indeed the hallmark of adulthood – in comparison to childhood, when we would more correctly describe it as inner and outer being and experience, neither of which is open to informed choice by the child but more or less left to providence and parental guidance. This also indicates why children need to be brought up, to that realm of *within-and-without reality*, which will not come about if they are left to their own devices. When we observe how even very young children continually experiment, more or less playfully, as from one day to the next they move and are moved closer to maturity, we correctly conclude that the desire for maturity exists, as a growth-factor, if you like, and as a result we understand more clearly what the motivations and limitations of our parental influence can be and are.

It seems we are quite right then to take rather seriously our liberty, as adults, to move at will between within and without ourselves, both inwardly and outwardly informed and occupied. We would not be doing justice, however, to our understanding of adulthood if we did not mention, along with the possible certainty of ourselves within, the initially unavoidable ambiguity and ambivalence of that which we come to experience without ourselves. The English language is always marvellous in this respect because it illustrates so finely the workings of our human being. When we describe something as 'outside' ourselves, we presuppose a barrier of sorts between ourselves and it, which might or might not be broken down. However that which is 'without' us is not barred from us but it is with us, albeit not inwardly but only outwardly. As adults therefore we run the risk, the healthy risk, of making the mistake that something exists 'out there' which is separate and divorced from us even while not barred from us. (In truth, of course, there is no such thing.) At times this ambiguity and ambivalence occurs to us as both difficult and fascinating. What we can take for granted is that it must always be up to us to opt for mature growth as we choose the *withness* and reject the *outness* of what is not within us. This ongoing 'yes, yes' and 'no, no' is implied by *adult maturation.* What we say yes to (the reality and beauty) enters into wholeness and completeness with what we certainly possess within ourselves, while what we say no to (the foreignness and strangeness) is outright unsuitable or merely not yet suitable.

A **maturing adult**, then, will first of all seek that universal order within himself, even as he repents of all false choices he has made until then. He has to become, to some extent, familiar with that universal order even before he can make any valid world choices, so he will seek out others who are equally desirous of learning about that universal order, which is not limited to individuals at a time but embraces all those who seek it out and find it. Then he will be able to say: 'This order is within and among us' and for the rest of his existence on earth he will be able to become more and more acquainted with it.

Meanwhile, on the basis of this foundation, he learns to distinguish between world that is real and beautiful and world that occurs to him as foreign and strange, ambiguous and ambivalent, difficult and fascinating, and then he says yes to the former and no to the latter. Maturity at this stage implies discernment, therefore, and what we might profitably call *worship in beauty and reality*. Meanwhile, separating sense from nonsense is important but not enough. It must lead to truthful works.

We can arrive at a crucial distinction here. First of all there is such a thing as *criticism*, which is mere discernment, when we can indeed tell between beauty and reality on one hand and what is foreign and strange on the other hand, but we do not make a practical choice. We do not say yes to the one and no to the other. *A critique*, by comparison, is more than mere criticism because creative work is involved that illustrates the difference between the two and recommends the choice of the former.

Criticism is always immature, because it is like a short-circuit in human endeavour. Then there is the thing called extinction, when we choose to busy ourselves with what we wrongly suppose exists beyond human recognition, so that we spend our time in pursuit of what is foreign and strange, ambiguous and ambivalent, difficult and fascinating. The satisfaction to be gained from that is deplorable. It is the food of ambition, the thrill of merely material and technical progress and the source of both popularity and magic. It is the broad road which leads to destruction. Those who take this road are never mature, they only get old.

Basically then, an **adult** is at liberty to choose from among creativity, extinction and criticism. Creativity is the narrow road and few take it. Extinction is the broad road travelled by most. Criticism is no road at all but more like an infatuation with the fork in the road.

We have said that even as an adult is not necessarily mature, so is a child not necessarily young, because **youth** is readily wasted, forfeited or betrayed. Immature adults will hanker after youth because they are afraid of getting old, even though the only way to prevent themselves from getting old would be if they continue to mature. What an immature adult is liable to seek in youth is the time when much was still possible which is no longer possible.

*

Youth, true youth, is never quite devoid of *the illusion of immortality*; we might even say that it is due to such an illusion. There is good reason for this illusion. We are given a taste of immortality while we are young so that we will seek and attain to the reality of it as adults. This is like being in love so that we will learn to love. By illusion I do not mean delusion. We are not deluded in our youth but we harbour the illusion of immortality. Our **youth is wasted, forfeited and betrayed** if no proper attention is paid to this illusion by those who possess the reality of it.

The illusions of immortality of the young must fade before actual immortality can be acquired. We might say that the illusions of immorality must die. In the same way the illusory feelings and thoughts of love, when we have fallen in love, must be given up if we are to learn to love unconditionally.

The 'young adult', or adolescent, unavoidably makes the acquaintance of a death of sorts as those illusions of immortality separate off from him. It is the same process of dying that is experienced by him who was in love and now learns to love. An awareness of actual immortality and practice of unconditional love however soon enough amount to eternal life, so that what we have is a simultaneous dying and living again, which is the hallmark of maturing human beings. There is a dying to youth and a living again in maturity. No one who experiences maturity like this regrets losing his youth.

We arrive at the gates of adulthood and are terrified by the demands the world makes on us. Or we leap into extinction because it deadens our mind and soul at least temporarily to thoughts of approaching death. Approaching adulthood to a child can in a way be like approaching death to an adult. A mature adult will not fear death because he knows it as transformation of one sort or another. A child on the threshold of adulthood, a youth, in other words, if his youth is in tact, is not afraid of adulthood for that same reason. In various cultures celebrations and rites

61

of passage mark these periods of transformation, but the entire upbringing of a child will surely always benefit from the examples of adult maturity set him by parental adults in his environment. As a young child turns into a young man or a young woman, he or she becomes more and more acquainted with creative measures that bring world into perspective. The productive attitude towards pain and death, towards all kinds of inconvenience and discomfort, has been nourished over many years and the visible reward for successful childish endeavour is gradually replaced by the invisible reward for active good spirit. A mature human being knows the full satisfaction of inward success, while external success as such no longer brings him contentment.

A child's **youth is forfeited** if that child is forced into adult ways and means. As immature adults we try to turn children into the beings we wish we ourselves still were. This is of course disastrous for them. Or we train them to behave like adults, which means that we train them to behave like immature adults, since a mature adult would not do that to a child. If the immature adult favours extinction we have the worst of all possible worlds.

At this stage we should perhaps ask: If children are raised, do they still need to be **schooled**? If they are not properly brought up, they need to that extent to be **educated**, which simply means that what has been neglected in terms of upbringing is caught up by way of education. Schooling as a kind of training can of course be a useful aspect of such corrective education but then it refers to various remedial or even curative approaches to a child that is bewildered or psychically in chaos. Such schooling must always be educative in principle and not like animal training. The mind boggles when we try to imagine how many of the so-called attainments of civilization would have to be ignored if a child were to be properly educated out of a state of insufficient upbringing. According to conventional perception, education and schooling are preparations for existence and survival in a competitive Society under the constant pressures and stresses of materialistic and spiritualistic success and economic progress. All too often, therefore, it is simply a misguiding of children, into extinction.

It's true enough that if our own childhood has been deprived of sufficient youth in the past, then there is no reason why we should not turn to young children in order to learn from them. We can become 'like little children'. Instinctively we can absorb the certainty that is based on human natural faith and trust. We simply ignore all our immaturities and bathe in youthful illusion. We have been too certainly wrong, too mistakenly certain. This certainty is dissolved when we empathize with how a child plays at being sure. Our human natural ease and levity must be rediscovered so that the measure of our own childhood might be filled at this late date. Only then can we set out into mature adulthood on the right footing. In other words if our own youth has been forfeited, we are able to recapture it if we become like young children. Not like children whose youth has been wasted, forfeited or betrayed but like young children. Then, if ever we have children of our own or are able in some other way to be parentally influential, we will understand that youth is precious inasmuch as it streams into maturity as into an ocean, while we lead and guide.

Youth is betrayed by those who wilfully ignore it and do not allow it to exist. Who would do such a thing? Why would anyone do such a thing? Would we do that out of revenge for having had our own youth betrayed?

What I have called the illusion of immortality, which is such an important aspect of being young, can seem to us immature adults like a mockery, like a falsehood, like culpable gullibility. We feel we need to stamp it out because we are scandalized in our state of adult abstraction. We wait until the child is once again displaying simplicity of means and motive and come down hard on any evidence of this, in the interest – I hate to mention it – of some ideal or false god.

Inasmuch as we are disciplinarians and moralists we betray youth. Its playful experimentation and its illusion of immortality seem to run counter to our idea of independence and self-control. What does not help, of course, is that the idea of youthfulness becomes fashionable among immature adults, when the sole alternative seems to be to get old. Youth should never be seen as an end in itself but always as the natural determinant of future development. As an ideal, again, youth is resented, and betrayed, by those who cannot find their way into a mature way of life. We have to understand that just as maturity makes demands on us, so does youth present us with obligations. The young are regularly reminded, by negative thought and emotion, of the fact that their youth is a transient state, however it is up to mature adults to remind them that maturity is positively great. There is no better time to remind them than when those negative thoughts and emotions beset them.

Presenting children with the delusion of an eternally happy childhood is also a betrayal of their youth. That notion of 'letting the child be happy and carefree because the onerous cares and problems of adulthood arrive all too soon' is a philistine invention which debilitates, by way of shame and guilt, that readiness of the child for dealing with unavoidable and unpleasant changes. The good parent is the one who is on the look-out for onsets of misery in the child, so that he can take the opportunity for implanting seeds of spiritual growth, not the one who tries to anticipate and prevent unhappiness at any cost. Alas, how thoroughly must we not overcome our own resentment at having had our youth betrayed before we can take such opportunities! The worst of it is that in our ambition to appear competent as parents we repress such resentment and pretend that it does not exist. As a consequence that vicious circle develops, where a parent makes children pay for his or her own unconscious impairments.

*

Adolescence, or 'young adulthood', is a term commonly used for the period of growth just prior to adulthood proper. The child has been nourished and is now beginning to nourish him- or herself. It is also a term that indicates a peculiarly problematic state of a child, when he frequently seems no longer young and not yet mature. There is no need for a crisis, since growing up can dovetail smoothly into being grown up but when the transition becomes critical, what needs to be looked at is the child's state of youth and his expectations of adulthood and maturity. When youth, due to mistreatment or insufficient upbringing, has separated from childhood, then we should expect a similar separation, in the child's mind, of maturity from adulthood. Nothing is more unbearable for a child near the end of his childhood than to harbour a vision of adulthood as necessarily immature. It is not enough, however, to try to repair that vision. What needs to be repaired first, or at least at the same time, is the young child. We should not allow ourselves to be overly swayed by the age of the child. If the measure of childhood is not full, as we indicated above, adulthood will assert itself all the same but not on a solid foundation. We have to keep in mind that the change from child to adult is a matter of physical necessity and the timing of the change, in any given case, is neither up to us nor up to the child in question. The child's change-over from youth to maturity, however, is up to us, the parental adults. The child grows up, to adulthood; we as the parental adults bring up, to maturity.

The education of adolescents is therefore especially interesting because the nearly adult child has a vision, an idea, a notion and no doubt a set of opinions regarding adulthood, especially on account of an increasing consciousness that adulthood is unavoidable. Maturity is avoidable, but not adulthood. Maturity makes adulthood desirable but immaturity is bound to cause it to appear as a threat to the child. While the child is afraid of adulthood, to the extent that he associates it with immaturity because the only adults that have been around him have been immature, it is not very likely that his childhood will come to a successful closure.

We can understand why the proper education of adolescents is all too commonly avoided by adults because during the course of it the adult's own immaturity is bound to become highlighted. As a consequence the problems peculiar to adolescence are fudged and falsified. Especially the functionaries in the pay of educational institutions, who are mistakenly called teachers and profess to 'prepare the child for life', are singularly ill equipped for truly educating adolescent children because any maturity of which they may once have been capable has been displaced by professionalism. As if it were not enough that a child's youth has been wasted, forfeited and betrayed, now the child is trained to resent youth itself, as something that prevents him from embracing adulthood, which is no way to repair and heal the young child.

Let those who teach always see to their own maturity first. **Maturity** implies creativity. The essence of **creativity** is the imaginative overcoming of hindrances to growth. The growth of a mature adult is spiritual. The adult cooperates with merciful spirit throughout during the acquisition of greater wisdom. Hindrances to growth are seen by him as counterproductive, which means that these hindrances stimulate while at the same time presenting a risk. Although pain may be involved, progress need not be anything other than easy.

Mature adults, as they wish to grow, will naturally seek the company of those who might benefit from their mature example. They are, by choice, sympathetic and compassionate. By being creative they overcome in themselves the hindrances to their growth that are due to voluntary exposure both to children who are in need of education (of repair, due to negligent upbringing) and to immature adults who are in need of adult education, (of repair due to a lack of wisdom).

A mature adult's creativity can go on inwardly only or both inwardly and outwardly. (It cannot go on outwardly only.) This creativity in action is called work. We say rightly that it goes on but it is also done. We indicated this above by mentioning the cooperation with merciful spirit. This spirit supplies measure and mastery. We supply good will and initiative.

Creative works are always examples of mature human being plus indications of how such maturity can be achieved. Ease, levity, leisure and luxury can all be hallmarks of creative works. Magic, however, spoils.

It would be wrong to suppose that what we create inwardly alone is solely for our own benefit. He who quietly forgives an insult certainly benefits himself but his behaviour may also be of benefit to the one who insulted him if that person allows himself to be touched by that creative act. If he does not, this takes nothing away from what the one who forgave him gains.

Creative works that also exist outwardly can also be called art works. However if the inward connection is lost, what we have is magic. If that connection is intentionally rejected, we end up with sorcery. Magic and sorcery spoil and pervert.

If the inward, individual man is true, the outward, personal man will be real. Both the truth and the reality of a human being are evident in his or her works. The inward works are "the better part". Outward works are wholly good. Let him who understands this take it to heart.

*

A few words about gender and sex now. These can turn into extremely complicated issues but we will have to make do here with a few pointers, as for example:

To be **male** is not the same as being **a male**. To be **female** is not the same as being **a female**.

We are born either male or female. The difference between the two is both essential and existential. By that I mean that gender difference does not exist only in terms of conduct and behaviour but also on the basis of inherited traits. Male inherited traits are world oriented while female inherited traits pertain to community. This is so even before male and female human beings are aware of each other. These traits however do not become operative and they are not effective until a degree of **masculinity** and **femininity** has been brought into being. Until then these traits lie dormant.

In the meanwhile what happens and is likely to happen is what is usually called the war of the sexes. Those of either gender suppose that sexuality is a viable proposition. Adolescents and adults alike may suppose as much. What I mean by sexuality is the assumption that maleness in isolation or femaleness in isolation is worth sustaining, even throughout life. The gender traits do not, however enter into this. What it amounts to is that both male and female individuals, in separation, get the idea that a merely outward expression of maleness or femaleness, in ignorance of the above mentioned traits, should be possible. Poorly brought up adolescents can fall into this trap as readily as immature adults. The path towards manhood and womanhood is of course laid out potentially in our make-up but what matters is how we believe, or how we are led to believe, that this path may be taken. Even in children we may observe this unfortunate trend, that a boy has come to rely on his maleness to define himself and a girl has come to depend on her femaleness for her identity. In such cases even boys and girls, barely brought up, resist and exclude each other. In the company of immature adults, whose sexuality has become ingrained, what else can we expect from those children? We can imagine what happens if the opposition is too strong. If a child's mistaken reliance on his (or her) sex is overwhelmed by the mistaken reliance on sex of the immature adults around him, it is bound to seem to him that he has no choice but to give up the struggle in that direction. Unfortunately he may suppose he is giving up a great deal, when in fact it merely becomes clear in his case that maleness as such, and in the case of a girl femaleness as such, cannot be sustained. What is required is the coordination of those gender traits we mentioned above.

We said that these gender traits lie dormant – which implies that they can be accessed. The question now is how this can be done. The struggle for sustained maleness and femaleness is the selfish (hedonistic) concern of individuals in their own exclusive interest and while they continue to pursue that interest, those gender traits remain in abeyance. While adults are still ignorant of those gender traits, we are right to describe them as males and females, not as male or female human beings or as men and women.

How, then, can those gender traits come to, or be brought to, our attention? One important fact is that we cannot come up with the knowledge ourselves, by way of self-analysis, meditation or reflection or such like. Gender traits can only come to our consciousness, and then to our awareness, by way of interaction with the other 'sex'. As boys and girls interact, under the umbrella of mature parentage and in the company of parental adults, in other words while they are being brought up, and specifically as they are taught and learn to **honour the other sex**, their gender traits come to the fore in each. We speak quite rightly of 'the other sex' – even of 'the opposite sex' if things have deteriorated to that extent – prior to any learned knowledge of how this sexual selfishness can be overcome. Only with every instance of overcoming does gender trait consciousness and later awareness come into being.

As children grow up towards adulthood we can take it for granted that their maleness and femaleness as sexuality will again and again, even in the mere presence of the other sex, occur to them, be it as a force or as a constraint. Each time they will either be misled into supposing that such forces and constraints are viable so that they will experience a dubious success or defeat on those terms, or – they will be brought up to know that honourable behaviour and conduct towards the 'other sex', and especially towards the supposedly 'opposite sex', brings to the surface something that can be sustained and is worthy of being sustained, namely **gender traits**, which is to say **world awareness in the case of the male human being and community awareness in the case of the female human being**. With every such instance the likelihood that the concerned human being will misdevelop as a male or a female will somewhat diminish.

World and community are not mutually exclusive domains but awareness of community readily leads to world awareness, while world awareness can include community awareness. Whether it does so or not depends in either case on the degree of **gender concourse**.

We can see how in order for world and community to be genuinely known and appreciated, male and female human beings not in isolation but in concourse are required. It is only by way of such concourse that the gender traits dormant from birth can gradually become relevant

We might speak of <u>sexual selfishness</u> in comparison to <u>gender care</u>. Males and females are egotists. As males or as females we are egotists and ignorant of how to serve our own best interests. We do not realize that we must do it through another and through others. Egotistic, or selfish, interest has a bearing exclusively on ourselves and therefore on our selves. As soon as we learn to take care of another or of others, there wells up in us a courage for life and this is essential if we are to make a go of things. As egotists we have no notion of life and certainly not the courage for it. When we come across it we stamp it out because it threatens our mistaken belief in ourselves as desirably independent of others (anti-communal) and somehow in control of the world (anti-world). While we pursue this independence and control as a goal we come no closer to manhood and womanhood. We remain ignorant of our gender and gradually wear ourselves out sexually. This is most unfortunate and oh how we wish we had been enlightened! How we wish we had sought wisdom rather than selfish satisfaction!

It is never too late.

So it is caring concourse with members of the 'other sex' that reveals to us our ability to care for world, if we are male, or to care for community, if we are female. Those abilities would not occur to us if we only had concourse with members of our 'own sex'.[1]

Parental adults who keep this in mind will have more success with bringing up and educating children. Remember that upbringing, in this respect of sex and gender, involves concern first and foremost for the inculcation of an habitual sense of honour in relation to the other sex, while education means repair wherever hindrances to this sense have developed.

In conclusion then we might say that masculinity and femininity pertain not to sexual intercourse, which is basically selfish, but to gender concourse, which is honourable and caring. And should we suppose that anything at all that is honourable and caring should be excluded from gender concourse? No, nothing at all.

*

The sooner we stop pretending that what can go on in modern schools is education, the sooner will we find time for that repair where it should and can in fact go on, namely at home, in community. It will also mean that per-

---

[1] Perhaps this as good a place as any to remind that maturity is not a state but the definition of how we evolve. Therefore if we suppose we ought to limit our care to those who are equally as mature as ourselves, we are on the wrong track. In fact we become more mature by taking a caring interest both in the development of the young and in the education of immature adults. Our maturity would decline if we cloistered ourselves with members supposedly of our own degree of gender awareness.

sonal schooling is possible more honestly and modestly within the means that are practicable in some particular neighbourhood, as training, instruction and exercise. While we suppose that education can go on institutionally, professionally and impersonally, parental adults will be misled into ignoring their own educational tasks, which must accompany the child's upbringing. Any truly parental adult brings up and educates children in person. At the same time any adult can train, instruct and exercise children in line with his or her own abilities and skills. It stands to reason that beyond that, under the guidance of instructors, who are especially informed, specific skills can be exercised, information can be imparted, training and instruction can quite readily go on in a group, because collective attention is focussed not inwardly on the communal and world relationship of a person, which is the province of upbringing and education but outwardly on the acquisition of a few work-related organs, faculties and efficiencies. If the upbringing and education, as delivered by parental adults, has not been neglected but pursued with dedication and in a loving spirit, then the schooling is bound to proceed as a matter of course and will no longer have to be institutionally initiated, supported and enforced by the State.

All the emphasis must therefore be placed on the work done by parental adults. Remember, they are adults who know that their maturity depends in part on the responsibility they assume for children in their family and community.

What, then, is a **teacher**, in terms of upbringing, education and schooling? He shows us how to do all these. He is gifted with the ability to grasp the essence of interpersonal relationship and to communicate this essence, in a great variety of ways, as are most suitable at the time in his community.

It cannot surprise us that all these terms we have mentioned refer to interrelated entities. Childhood, youth, adolescence, adulthood, maturity, parenthood and then sexuality, gender, male and female, manhood and womanhood – all these concern us when we choose to care for human beings, thereby equally taking care of ourselves. If we try to take care of ourselves without taking care of others we end up taking care of our *selves* and become isolated from world and community.

The question might arise: What if no one wants to be taken care of? What if we live entirely among people who are hell-bent on their individually independent pursuits of health and happiness? Certainly one can imagine that the times might come round to that.

In that case all is contained, of our effort and effectiveness, in the offer we make and in the opportunities we create. Why should we wait, if we want to be creative, until the time is right? No, the time is always right and an able talent will prove itself even in hell. A mature human being will not look around and wish for the world to be different but he will see 'world' as it is and shape his character accordingly.

It remains for us to take a look at what it means when we get **old**. We have indicated that being young and youth is the province of children, when the illusion of immortality prepares human beings for the real immortality of their mature years.

Age and being old, in comparison to youth and being young, is what mature adults say no to, just as they say yes to youth and being young in the children for whom they have accepted parental responsibility. The only way we can avoid getting old however is by continuing to mature, by continuing to worship in reality, by continuing to work in terms of true world beauty and reality, which of course presupposes the nourishment of our inward being.

As soon as we mature we also risk getting old because maturation implies an exposure to the supposed foreignness and strangeness of world, even while its beauty and reality appeals to us. That appeal becomes less effective in proportion to the active interest we take in what seems to exist as foreign and strange, as ambiguous and ambivalent, as difficult and fascinating. Eventually we no longer see world at all but merely the mythic world and then 'this world'. Of course if the youth of childhood was wasted, forfeited and betrayed, the adult in question may never have come into contact with world as beauty and reality at all. When a child is not brought up, and then not educated so that this lack of upbringing might be repaired, that individual may have been exposed to nothing but training, instruction and exercise and even that would then have been administered in a wrong, if not bad, spirit, well, in that case can we expect any maturation at all? Which is not to say that the unfortunate individual, tragically crippled in his childhood, might not turn into a brilliant manipulator of 'this world', a veritable stupor mundi. There seems to be no end to 'the great wonders' an extinct intellect can come up with, either on account of misdirected maturity or in terms of chronic immaturity. Whatever it is, it is certainly **old**.

We might do well, as an afterthought, to distinguish between **old** and **ancient** and also between **old** and **age**. That which belongs to a former time is ancient. An art worker, for example, will always, so to speak, deal in both present time and former time because his intention is to show how beauty and realty of world is 'time-honoured' and not merely fashionable or nostalgic. Among those, in the past, who have dedicated themselves to the cultivation of human intelligence and feeling, there have been those who stressed the importance of ancient values in order to get away from those that are corrupt and modern. The contemporary quality of life depends as much on how we perceive past time as on how we experience present time. 'Personal renewal', if that is a concept we can feel comfortable with, is therefore as much a revision of what is past as it is a disclosure of what is present. What is past, and patient of revision, should therefore be what we mean by **ancient being**, whereas the outcome especially of mature adulthood sacrificed to the pursuit of the wrongly supposed existence of strange and fascinating world, of unreal and ugly world, should be what we mean by **old being**.

This knowledge too would stand us in good stead as we construct our existential foundation.

* * * * *

(Oct.2007)

77

www.ingramcontent.com/pod-product-compliance
Lightning Source LLC
Chambersburg PA
CBHW070301290526
45791CB00003B/1032